OFFSIDE OR ON? THE DEFINITIVE GUIDE TO VAR IN FOOTBALL

Navigating the Controversies, Strategies, and Game-Changing Moments of Video Assistant Refereeing in the World's Most Beloved Sport

By

Matthew M. Hamilton

Copyright © 2024 by Matthew M. Hamilton

All rights reserved. No part of this publication may be reproduced, distributed, or transmitted in any form or by any means, including photocopying, recording, or other electronic or mechanical methods, without the prior written permission of the publisher, except in the case of brief quotations embodied in critical reviews and certain other noncommercial uses permitted by copyright law.

Disclaimer

The views and opinions expressed in this book are those of the author and do not necessarily reflect the official policy or position of any organization or entity mentioned. The information contained in this book is for general informational purposes only. While the author has made every attempt to ensure the accuracy and completeness of the information provided, the author makes no representations or warranties of any kind, express or implied, about the completeness, accuracy, reliability, suitability, or availability with respect to the contents of this book for any purpose. Any reliance you place on such information is therefore strictly at your own risk.

ABOUT THE AUTHOR

 Matthew M. Hamilton is an ardent football enthusiast and writer known for his insightful analysis of the sport's evolution, particularly in the realm of technology and officiating. With a background in sports journalism, Matthew brings a wealth of experience and a unique perspective to his writing. His passion for football shines through in his engaging prose, where he explores the intricacies of the game with depth and nuance. Whether dissecting the latest developments in Video Assistant Refereeing (VAR) or delving into tactical innovations, Matthew's work is characterized by its thoughtful analysis, meticulous research, and commitment to preserving the essence of the beautiful game while embracing its evolution in the digital age.

TABLE OF CONTENTS

INTRODUCTION.. 8
  Introducing the Conventional Refereeing System.. 10
  Presenting VAR: The Origins and Development of VAR.. 12
  The Promise and Danger: Preliminary Anticipations vs Actualities.............................. 14

TECHNOLOGY AND IMPLEMENTATION IN THE OPERATION OF VAR..16
  Process of Making Decisions: From Event to Review... 18
  Impact on Team Dynamics and Referee Communication in Officiating......................... 20

REVEALING DISPUTATIONS...........................23
  The Argument for and Against VAR................ 25
  Case Studies: High-Profile VAR Controversies... 27
  In this chapter, we examine a series of high-profile controversies that have thrust Video Assistant Refereeing (VAR) into the spotlight, dissecting the intricacies and implications of each incident on the world of football..............27
  Fan Reaction: From Jubilation to Frustration.. 29

TACTICAL ADAPTATIONS...............................32
  Managerial Strategies: Adapting to VAR.........34
  Player Mindset: Playing under the Shadow of Technology... 37
  Tactical Innovations: Exploiting VAR's Weaknesses and Strengths............................ 39

THE FUTURE OF VAR......................................42

Refinement and Improvement: Addressing Criticisms..44
VAR in International Competitions: Challenges and Opportunities...47
Predicting the Next Evolution: VAR 2.0 and Beyond..49

BEYOND THE PITCH..52
Officiating Ethics and Integrity.........................54
Financial Implications: VAR's Impact on Clubs and Leagues.. 57
Societal Reflections: VAR's Influence on Fan Culture and Football Discourse........................60

CONCLUSION..63
Lessons Learned: Reflecting on VAR's Journey. 65
Looking Ahead: Anticipating the Next Chapter in Football's Technological Evolution.............. 68
Final Thoughts: Balancing Tradition with Progress in the Beautiful Game......................71

INTRODUCTION

The implementation of Video Assistant Refereeing (VAR) has created a revolution in football history unlike anything before, as the game continues to change and every pass, tackle, and goal is examined closely by fans worldwide. What started out as an effort to improve the accuracy of the calls made by the referees has turned into a divisive force that is changing football itself.

We get deep into the core of VAR in this book, analyzing its history, workings, debates, and strategic ramifications. In the process of upending long-standing traditions and bringing in a new era of technological influence, VAR has made an enduring impression on sport, whether it be in the intimate stadiums of local leagues or the massive venues of international events.

As we examine VAR's workings, we reveal the complex procedures that control its application, illuminating the inner workings that have attracted and irritated stakeholders and fans alike. We peel back the layers of technology that have merged with the drama of matchday, from the painstaking analysis of critical moments to the intricate interactions between on-field referees and their video assistant counterparts.

VAR is not without controversy, though. We traverse the turbulent waters of discussion, delving into the divisive viewpoints and prominent occurrences that have brought VAR to the forefront. We explore the effects of VAR on the fundamentals of fair play and the emotional rollercoaster it causes for supporters worldwide, from contested goals to controversial red cards.

However, in the midst of the chaos, some tactical adjustments are being made. Teams innovate, players adapt, and managers strategize to take advantage of the unique opportunities and challenges that VAR presents. We reveal the tactical complexity that has surfaced, from taking advantage of VAR's shortcomings to realizing its promise as a transformative tool.

There are many unanswered questions as we look beyond. In what ways will VAR develop further? What effects might that have on football's financial situation and game integrity? What does the introduction of VAR mean for the ageless customs and unshakeable passions that characterize football? This is possibly the most significant question.

Come along with us as we dive deep into VAR, exploring everything from its origins to its potential future applications. With painstaking research, gripping tales, and knowledgeable commentary, we want to disentangle the intricacies of VAR and its significant influence on the most popular sport in the world.

Introducing the Conventional Refereeing System

Football was governed by a conventional refereeing system that had been refined over many years prior to the introduction of Video Assistant Refereeing (VAR). This chapter takes a step back to examine the underlying principles that formed the framework for officiating in the sport.

Football referees have always had a difficult time keeping the laws of the game fair because of the fast-paced action and split-second judgements that occur during games. From small-scale games played on muddy fields to major international competitions, referees have served as the arbiters of justice, responsible for rendering decisions that could decide the fate of a match in an instant.

We examine the function of the on-field referee, whose jurisdiction encompasses the whole field and who commands the difference and compliance of players, coaches, and fans in equal measure. Referees have to make their way through a flurry of activity, interpreting fouls, offsides, and other infractions in real time, relying solely on their eyes and ears.

Referees may be highly skilled and experienced, yet they are still fallible humans with subjectivity and error. Due to the speed of the game and the limitations of the human eye, controversial decisions were frequently made during football games, which led to unending discussions and disputes.

Still, the old-fashioned refereeing method persisted, rooted in history and valued for its directness and ease of use. Referees were held in high regard as the protectors of the game, charged with the grave responsibility of guaranteeing sportsmanship and fair play.

However, as the demands of contemporary football became more sophisticated, so did the need for increased precision and responsibility in officiating. A technological revolution was about to begin, one that would upend the fundamental basis of the current officiating system and usher in a new period of intense scrutiny known as "Video Assistant Refereeing."

Presenting VAR: The Origins and Development of VAR

This chapter chronicles the amazing development of Video Assistant Refereeing (VAR) from its conception to the world of football, when it was first implemented.

Growing demands for more precision and fairness in officiating led to the sowing of the seeds for video assistant ratiometry. A more dependable refereeing system was required as technology developed and football game stakes rose to previously unheard-of levels.

We explore the early trials and prototypes that served as the foundation for video assistant regulation (VAR), ranging from basic instant replay systems to complex video analysis tools. In the background, creative thinkers and technological experts put up endless effort to create a system that would complement rather than replace the on-field referee's duties.

Football history saw a sea change with the introduction of VAR, as the game adopted technology in ways never seen before. We examine the significant turning points and innovations that made video assistant refereeing (VAR) a reality, from its early testing in friendlies to its well-publicized global premiere.

But there were difficulties along the way as VAR developed. Football purists bemoaned the infiltration of technology into the game's age-old customs, while critics expressed worries about possible disruptions to the game's flow. However, supporters contended that VAR may improve the sport's fairness and integrity and usher in a new era of accountability and transparency.

The arguments around VAR's application developed along with it. We look at the various stances taken by various football leagues and administrations, ranging from the careful use of VAR in certain areas to its complete inclusion in others.

In the end, the development of VAR marks a turning point in the continuing history of football. VAR is proof of the persistent pursuit of greatness and justice on the field, even as the sport struggles with the challenges posed by tradition and technology.

The Promise and Danger: Preliminary Anticipations vs Actualities

In this chapter, we address the contradictory aspects of Video Assistant Refereeing (VAR) by weighing the great hopes it once had against the harsh realities it has faced since being implemented in the football globe.

When VAR was first introduced, it was heralded as a game-changer because it promised to correct grave mistakes, end injustices, and preserve the integrity of sports. In their ideal future, the skill and effort of the players on the pitch would be the only factors determining the result of games, and controversial decisions would become a thing of the past.

However, once VAR was incorporated into football, the promises it made ran counter to the subtleties and complexity of the actual game. We examine the original hopes for VAR, ranging from its ability to do away with blatant mistakes to its function in advancing justice and openness.

But the actual use of VAR has shown to be significantly more complex than expected. We must deal with the dangers and pitfalls that have surfaced, such as the disputed interpretations of

VAR rulings and the unforeseen effects on the tempo and flow of games. It became evident that not all of football's officiating issues had been handled by VAR as it got entangled in disputes and discussions.

However, amid the obstacles and critiques, there have also been encouraging signs. We present examples of how VAR has effectively fixed grave mistakes and offered certainty when things were unclear. We also look at the continuous efforts to hone and develop VAR, ranging from changes to the technology itself to improvements in official education and training.

In the end, VAR's potential and danger serve as a reminder of the difficulties involved in achieving football perfection. As the game continues to struggle with how technology may affect its age-old customs, VAR serves as a symbol of advancement as well as a warning about the unexpected outcomes that might occur when innovation and tradition collide on the sacred turf of the football pitch.

TECHNOLOGY AND IMPLEMENTATION IN THE OPERATION OF VAR

This chapter takes readers on a thorough exploration of the technological marvel known as Video Assistant Refereeing (VAR), including an examination of its complex workings and real-world applications on football fields.

We start by exploring the technology architecture that serves as VAR's core. We reveal the array of high-definition cameras placed thoughtfully throughout the stadium and the advanced video review systems housed within the VAR room. These hardware and software components allow VAR to accurately and precisely record, analyze, and decide on-field incidents.

Careful preparation and coordination are required for the seamless adoption of VAR into sport. We examine the practical difficulties in applying VAR in stadiums with different dimensions and layouts, from setting up camera systems to creating specialized VAR control rooms furnished with the newest gear for communication.

The smooth incorporation of VAR into the current officiating structure is essential to its efficacy. We look at the rules and guidelines that control how on-field referees and video assistant referees (VARs) interact, emphasizing the lines of communication and decision-making processes that allow for prompt and forceful involvement when needed.

However, VAR is not without its drawbacks and difficulties. We address the technical limitations and pragmatic issues that may affect the dependability and efficiency of VAR, ranging from the possibility of malfunctions to the subjective character of some officiating judgements.

We demonstrate the practical use of VAR in various leagues and competitions through case studies and real-world examples, highlighting its role in improving the fairness and accuracy of refereeing decisions. We also look at the continuous efforts to develop and enhance VAR technology, from new developments in camera technology to the creation of AI algorithms for automated judgment.

We get a greater understanding of the mutually beneficial interplay between technology and tradition in the world of football as we work through the complications of VAR. Virtual Assistant

Refereeing (VAR) is a paradigm shift in officiating, but its effective deployment depends on finding the ideal balance between innovation and upholding the fundamental principles of the sport.

Process of Making Decisions: From Event to Review

This chapter traces the path of an on-field incident from its occurrence to the final review and adjudication, providing a thorough examination of the decision-making process built into Video Assistant Refereeing (VAR).

First, we look at the critical points at which VAR intervention occurs. We reveal the standards used to choose when and how VAR is used to assess on-field situations, whether it be a contested goal, a possible penalty, or a contentious red card. We examine the difficulties and factors that affect the choice to ask for the VAR's help from the viewpoint of the on-field referee.

After an occurrence is selected for review, we examine the methods used by the VAR to carry out its investigation. We reveal the technologies and resources available to the VAR, like advanced replay systems and high-definition video recordings, which allow them to examine every facet of the occurrence with clarity and precision.

Nevertheless, the review itself is not the conclusion of the decision-making process. We examine the rules and guidelines that control the exchange of information between the VAR and the on-field referee, emphasizing the cooperative aspect of VAR intervention and the significance of precise and unambiguous communication in arriving at a judgment.

The idea of "clear and obvious errors" is essential to the decision-making process since it establishes the threshold for validating or overturning the referee's initial ruling. We disentangle the subtleties and interpretations that guide the VAR's evaluation of situations, delving into the subjectivity of some rulings and the difficulties in reaching an agreement.

We highlight the difficulties and challenges authorities have while using VAR through case studies and real-world instances. We draw attention to the various facets of VAR involvement and its influence on match results, including the need for quick decisions and the scrutiny of spectators, athletes, and commentators.

We learn more about how technology will affect football officiating in the future as we work our way through the VAR decision-making process. However, we also understand how critical it is to strike a balance between human judgment and technical advancement in order to make sure that VAR adds to rather than takes away from the integrity and spirit of the great game.

Impact on Team Dynamics and Referee Communication in Officiating

This chapter examines the significant effects of Video Assistant Refereeing (VAR) on officiating teams' dynamics, ranging from the exchange of information between on-field referees and VARs to the wider implications for cohesiveness and team dynamics.

Effective officiating is largely dependent on communication, and VAR changes this relationship. We examine the rules and guidelines that control communication between VARs and on-field referees, emphasizing the opportunities and difficulties that come with using this cooperative method of decision-making. We look at how VAR has changed the way officiating teams work together and communicate during games, from the usage of headset technology to the creation of clear lines of communication.

However, VAR's effects go beyond communication; they also have an impact on the larger dynamics among officiating teams. We examine how on-field referees' roles and responsibilities have changed since VAR was implemented, as they adjust to the more scrutiny and monitoring brought about by video technology. We also look at the mental and emotional toll that VAR rulings can have on referees as they deal with the strain of making snap decisions in front of players, spectators, and commentators.

We also take into account how VAR may affect officiating crew cohesion and team relations. We look into how officiating teams have become more accountable and collaborative as a result of VAR, as they cooperate to guarantee the justice and correctness of rulings. However, we also understand that differences between on-field officials and VARs can lead to tension and unrest, emphasizing the fine balance that needs to be found to preserve unity among officiating teams.

We highlight the difficulties and complexities of officiating in the VAR age using case studies and real-world instances. We offer insights into the

changing dynamics of officiating teams and the significant impact that VAR has had on their duties, responsibilities, and relationships, covering everything from the nuances of communication procedures to the psychological strains experienced by referees
.

We obtain a greater understanding of the intricacies of contemporary football officiating and the crucial role that excellent communication and teamwork play in maintaining the integrity and fairness of the beautiful game as we navigate through the effects of VAR on officiating dynamics.

REVEALING DISPUTATIONS

This chapter examines the debates surrounding Video Assistant Refereeing (VAR), from its conception to the football community's general acceptance of it. Due to the numerous arguments, conflicts, and controversies that have accompanied the adoption of video technology, controversy and VAR have practically become synonymous. We go deep into the core of these disputes, examining the divisive viewpoints and fervent debates that have broken out among supporters, athletes, coaches, and commentators.

The discussion around VAR centers on the relative merits of subjectivity and accuracy. We look at how different interpretations and assessments have led to a great deal of scrutiny and skepticism around VAR decisions, which are meant to remove blatant and obvious errors. We dissect the subtleties of VAR's influence on the tempo and flow of games, from offside judgements that depend on millimeters to handball rulings that provoke fury.

However, the debates surrounding VAR go beyond the specifics of decision-making and address more general concerns about honesty, fairness, and transparency. We look at how VAR has sparked concerns about the dependability and consistency of officiating as well as the possibility that outcomes could be influenced by prejudice or favoritism. We deal with the moral and ethical conundrums that occur when technology combines with the human drama of football, from apparent injustices that exacerbate fan ire to claims of VAR-induced gamesmanship.

There are, nevertheless, times when agreement and clarity prevail despite the disagreements. We present examples of when VAR has successfully fixed egregious mistakes and offered clarification during tense situations, reinstating confidence in the fairness of the game. In order to increase the efficacy and legitimacy of VAR, we also look at the ongoing attempts to hone and improve its protocols and procedures, responding to critiques and issues.

We demonstrate the complex nature of VAR disputes with case studies and real-world examples, ranging from well-publicized events that garner international notice to more localized conflicts that have a lasting impact on communities. We obtain a greater grasp of the difficulties and complexity involved in the quest of justice and fairness in the realm of football officiating as we work through the debates surrounding VAR.

The Argument for and Against VAR

This chapter examines the reasons for and against the use of Video Assistant Refereeing (VAR) in football, delving into the core of the current controversy around the technology.

The purported benefits and drawbacks of using video technology to officiate are at the center of the VAR controversy. We start by going over the possible advantages of VAR, such as its capacity to rectify blatantly obvious mistakes, improve the precision of officiating calls, and encourage equity and openness on the pitch. We look at how VAR has offered a vital second look at pivotal moments in games, from contested penalty calls to contentious offside calls, guaranteeing that results are decided by the letter of the law rather than by oversight or human mistake.

But in addition to its supporters, VAR has encountered strong opposition and criticism. We analyze the objections to VAR, focusing on issues such as how it would affect the tempo and flow of games, how subjective some of the rulings will be, and how technological errors could compromise the fairness of the competition. We examine the ways that VAR has prompted concerns about the fundamentals and spirit of football, from delays in decision-making to the deterioration of spontaneity and emotion.

However, throughout the debate, there are complex viewpoints to take into account. We look at the differing viewpoints across the football community, from coaches and officials to players and supporters, illuminating the subtleties and complexities that underlie the VAR controversy. We also look at the geographical differences in the use of VAR and the global lessons that may be drawn from various strategies and experiences.

We demonstrate the complex nature of the VAR discussion with case studies and real-world examples, ranging from high-profile events that garner international attention to more localized conflicts that strike a chord with communities. We obtain a greater grasp of the difficulties and complexity involved in the quest of justice and fairness in the realm of football officiating as we weigh the benefits and drawbacks of video assistant refereeing. In the end, the VAR controversy highlights the ongoing conflict between modernity and tradition as the sport struggles to understand how technology will affect its ageless customs and essential principles.

Case Studies: High-Profile VAR Controversies

In this chapter, we examine a series of high-profile controversies that have thrust Video Assistant Refereeing (VAR) into the spotlight, dissecting the intricacies and implications of each incident on the world of football.

The Handball Debate: We delve into the contentious issue of handball decisions and how VAR has amplified debates surrounding this aspect of the game. From penalties awarded for inadvertent handball to the interpretation of the handball law, we explore how VAR has reshaped perceptions of fairness and consistency in officiating.

Offside Calls Under Scrutiny: Offside decisions have long been a source of contention in football, and VAR has only heightened the scrutiny surrounding these calls. We analyze controversial offside decisions that have divided opinion among fans, players, and pundits, examining the complexities of determining offside with the aid of video technology.

Penalty Drama: VAR's role in awarding penalties – and overturning them – has sparked heated debates and raised questions about the threshold for VAR intervention. We dissect penalty incidents that have led to uproar and controversy, shedding light on the challenges of applying VAR to subjective decisions within the penalty area.

Red Card Reversals: The use of VAR to review red card decisions has been met with both praise and criticism, as the technology offers referees the opportunity to reconsider their initial judgments. We explore cases where red cards have been rescinded or upheld following VAR intervention, examining the impact on match outcomes and player discipline.

Goal Disallowed: Few incidents evoke as much emotion and controversy as a disallowed goal, and VAR has become a central player in these debates. We analyze instances where goals have been ruled out due to VAR reviews, exploring the implications for teams and the wider footballing community.

Through these case studies, we provide a comprehensive overview of the complexities and controversies inherent in VAR implementation. Each incident serves as a microcosm of the broader debates surrounding VAR, highlighting the challenges and opportunities presented by technology in the pursuit of fairness and accuracy in football officiating. As we navigate through these high-profile controversies, we gain a deeper understanding of the nuances and intricacies of VAR's impact on the beautiful game.

Fan Reaction: From Jubilation to Frustration

In this chapter, we explore the diverse spectrum of fan reactions to Video Assistant Refereeing (VAR), from moments of jubilation to instances of frustration and disillusionment.

The Joy of Justice: For some fans, VAR represents a beacon of hope, a symbol of progress in the pursuit of fairness and transparency in football officiating. We delve into the elation and relief experienced by supporters when VAR corrects a perceived injustice, overturning a controversial decision or awarding a crucial penalty in their team's favor. Through anecdotes and testimonials, we capture the raw emotion and euphoria that accompany moments of VAR-induced justice on the pitch.

The Agony of Injustice: Conversely, VAR has also been the source of heartbreak and despair for many fans, as controversial decisions and lengthy delays disrupt the flow and rhythm of matches. We examine the frustration and disillusionment felt by supporters when VAR overturns a goal or awards a penalty against their team, leaving them questioning the fairness and integrity of the officiating process. Through fan reactions captured in stadiums, on social media, and in fan forums, we illustrate the profound impact of VAR controversies on the emotional rollercoaster experienced by football fans.

The Quest for Consistency: Amidst the highs and lows of fan reactions to VAR, there is a common desire for consistency and clarity in officiating decisions. We explore the calls for greater transparency and accountability in VAR implementation, as fans seek reassurance that VAR interventions are conducted with integrity and impartiality. Through surveys and interviews, we gauge the level of trust and confidence that fans have in VAR and its ability to enhance – rather than detract from – the spectator experience.

Navigating the New Normal: As VAR becomes increasingly integrated into the fabric of football, fans are forced to adapt to a new reality where technology plays an ever-expanding role in the game. We examine the ways in which fans are embracing – or resisting – this shift, from debates over the impact of VAR on the atmosphere in stadiums to discussions about the future implications of technology on the sport's timeless traditions.

Through these diverse perspectives and reactions, we gain a deeper understanding of the complex relationship between fans and VAR, and the profound influence that technology has on the emotional experience of football fandom. As we navigate through the highs and lows of fan reactions to VAR, we recognize the enduring passion and devotion that unites football supporters around the world, transcending the controversies and challenges of modern officiating.

TACTICAL ADAPTATIONS

In this chapter, we explore the tactical landscape of football in the era of Video Assistant Refereeing (VAR), analyzing the strategic adjustments made by managers, players, and teams in response to the introduction of video technology.

Managerial Strategies: We examine how managers have adapted their tactics and game plans to navigate the challenges and opportunities presented by VAR. From proactive approaches aimed at exploiting VAR's weaknesses to reactive strategies focused on minimizing the risk of contentious decisions, we dissect the tactical innovations that have emerged on the sidelines.

Player Mindset: The introduction of VAR has not only impacted managers and coaches but also the mindset and approach of players on the pitch. We explore how players have adjusted their behavior and decision-making in light of VAR's presence, from altering their tackling technique to refraining from appealing for marginal calls. Through interviews and insights from players, we uncover the psychological and tactical factors that influence their performance in the VAR era.

Tactical Innovations: VAR has prompted teams to rethink traditional strategies and explore new avenues for gaining a competitive edge. We analyze the tactical innovations that have emerged, from set-piece routines designed to exploit VAR's scrutiny to defensive formations optimized to minimize the risk of conceding penalties. Through video analysis and tactical breakdowns, we reveal the intricacies of these adaptations and their impact on match dynamics.

Game Management: In addition to shaping tactics and strategy, VAR has also influenced the way teams manage games and control momentum. We explore how VAR decisions – whether favorable or unfavorable – can alter the course of a match, prompting teams to adjust their approach in real-time. From time-wasting tactics to strategic substitutions, we examine the tactical nuances of game management in the VAR era.

Through these tactical adaptations, we gain a deeper understanding of the dynamic interplay between technology and strategy in modern football. As managers, players, and teams navigate the complexities of VAR, they are forced to innovate and evolve, shaping the tactical landscape of the beautiful game in ways that were previously unimaginable. As we delve into the tactical adaptations of the VAR era, we uncover the ingenuity and creativity that define football's ever-evolving tactical evolution.

Managerial Strategies: Adapting to VAR

In this chapter, we delve into the intricate world of managerial strategies in response to the introduction of Video Assistant Refereeing (VAR) in football. Managers, the masterminds behind their teams' on-field performances, have had to navigate the challenges and opportunities presented by VAR, reshaping their tactical approaches and game plans accordingly.

Pre-Match Preparation: We explore how managers have incorporated VAR considerations into their pre-match preparations. From analyzing opponents' tendencies to studying VAR trends and tendencies, we uncover the meticulous planning and strategizing that goes into preparing for VAR-influenced matches.

In-Game Adjustments: The dynamic nature of football means that managers must be prepared to adapt their tactics and strategies on the fly. We examine how managers have adjusted their in-game tactics in response to VAR decisions, from making timely substitutions to tweaking formations to exploit VAR-induced vulnerabilities in the opposition.

Psychological Management: VAR's impact extends beyond the tactical realm, influencing the psychological mindset of both managers and players. We explore how managers have managed the psychological implications of VAR, from instilling resilience and focus in their players to maintaining composure and adaptability on the sidelines.

Post-Match Analysis: The advent of VAR has reshaped the post-match analysis process, as managers dissect VAR decisions and their impact on match outcomes. We analyze how managers have utilized VAR data and insights to inform their post-match assessments, identifying areas for improvement and refining their strategies for future matches.

Through case studies and interviews with leading managers, we uncover the diverse approaches taken to adapt to VAR and its influence on managerial decision-making. From pragmatic approaches aimed at minimizing the risk of VAR-induced setbacks to proactive strategies designed to exploit VAR-induced vulnerabilities in the opposition, we explore the tactical nuances of managerial adaptation in the VAR era.

As we delve into the managerial strategies employed in response to VAR, we gain a deeper appreciation for the role of managers as tacticians, strategists, and motivators in navigating the complexities of modern football officiating.

Player Mindset: Playing under the Shadow of Technology

In this chapter, we delve into the psychological and tactical dimensions of how players adapt to the presence of Video Assistant Refereeing (VAR) in football. The introduction of VAR has not only altered the dynamics of officiating but also influenced the mindset and behavior of players on the pitch.

Awareness and Adaptation: We explore how players have become increasingly aware of the presence of VAR and its potential impact on their actions during matches. From adapting their tackling technique to avoiding contentious challenges, players must navigate the fine line between aggression and caution in the VAR era. Through interviews and insights from players, we uncover the thought processes and strategies they employ to adjust to the heightened scrutiny of VAR.

Decision-Making Under Pressure: VAR introduces a new layer of pressure and scrutiny for players, as every action and decision is subject to review and analysis. We examine how players manage the psychological challenges of playing under the shadow of technology, from maintaining focus and concentration to controlling emotions and avoiding rash decisions that could result in VAR interventions.

Reframing Perspectives: The presence of VAR has forced players to reconsider their perspectives on officiating and fairness in football. We explore how players perceive the role of VAR in the game, from viewing it as a tool for justice and transparency to questioning its impact on the spontaneity and emotion of football. Through anecdotes and testimonials, we capture the diverse range of attitudes and opinions among players towards VAR and its influence on the game.

Adapting to Change: As technology continues to shape the landscape of football, players must adapt to the evolving demands and challenges of the modern game. We analyze how players embrace innovation and technology while maintaining the core values and traditions of football. From incorporating video analysis into their training routines to embracing VAR as a means of improving the integrity of the sport, we explore the ways in which players navigate the intersection of tradition and progress in the VAR era.

Through these insights into the player mindset in the shadow of technology, we gain a deeper understanding of the psychological and tactical dimensions of playing in the VAR era. As players grapple with the challenges and opportunities presented by VAR, they continue to evolve and innovate, shaping the future of football on and off the pitch.

Tactical Innovations: Exploiting VAR's Weaknesses and Strengths

In this chapter, we delve into the strategic adaptations made by teams and managers to exploit both the weaknesses and strengths of Video Assistant Refereeing (VAR) in football.

Exploiting Weaknesses: Teams have identified vulnerabilities in VAR's implementation and have developed tactical innovations to exploit them. We examine how teams strategically manipulate VAR's limitations, such as the delay in decision-making or the subjective nature of certain calls, to gain a competitive advantage. From time-wasting tactics to strategic challenges aimed at disrupting the flow of play and triggering VAR reviews, we uncover the tactical nuances of exploiting VAR's weaknesses.

Maximizing Strengths: Conversely, teams have also sought to capitalize on VAR's strengths to enhance their tactical approach. We analyze how teams leverage VAR to their advantage, from using video technology to analyze opponents' weaknesses and tendencies to appealing for VAR reviews strategically to overturn unfavorable decisions. Through case studies and tactical breakdowns, we reveal the innovative ways in which teams utilize VAR as a tactical asset on the field.

Defensive Resilience: Defensively, teams have adjusted their tactics to minimize the risk of conceding penalties or committing fouls that could lead to VAR interventions. We explore how teams organize defensively to mitigate the impact of VAR, from maintaining disciplined positioning to avoiding risky challenges in the penalty area. Through video analysis and tactical insights, we uncover the strategic adjustments made by teams to defend effectively in the VAR era.

Attacking Opportunism: Offensively, teams have sought to exploit VAR's potential to overturn decisions in their favor. We examine how teams capitalize on VAR-induced uncertainties to create scoring opportunities, from appealing for penalties in the opposition's penalty area to exploiting defensive vulnerabilities exposed by VAR reviews. Through tactical analysis and player interviews, we uncover the strategic innovations made by teams to maximize their attacking potential in the VAR era.

Through these tactical innovations, we gain a deeper understanding of the strategic nuances of playing in the VAR era. As teams adapt their tactics and strategies to exploit both the weaknesses and strengths of VAR, they continue to innovate and evolve, shaping the future of football on the pitch.

THE FUTURE OF VAR

Technological Advancements: We examine how ongoing technological advancements may shape the evolution of VAR in the coming years. From improvements in camera technology to the development of artificial intelligence algorithms for automated decision-making, we explore the potential for future innovations to enhance the accuracy and efficiency of VAR systems.

Refinement of Protocols: As VAR continues to mature, we anticipate the refinement of protocols and procedures governing its implementation. We analyze how footballing authorities may seek to standardize VAR protocols across different leagues and competitions, fostering greater consistency and transparency in officiating decisions.

Integration with Other Technologies: We explore the potential for VAR to integrate with other emerging technologies, such as augmented reality and player tracking systems. From enhancing the viewing experience for fans to providing real-time insights for coaches and analysts, we envision how the convergence of VAR with other technologies may revolutionize the way football is played and experienced.

Cultural and Ethical Considerations: Beyond technological advancements, we also consider the cultural and ethical implications of VAR's continued expansion. We examine how VAR may influence the traditions and values of footballing cultures around the world, as well as the potential ethical dilemmas that may arise from its widespread adoption.

Fan Engagement and Experience: Finally, we explore the implications of VAR on fan engagement and experience. From debates over the impact of VAR on the atmosphere in stadiums to discussions about its influence on the emotional rollercoaster of football fandom, we consider how VAR may shape the relationship between fans and the beautiful game in the years to come.

Through these reflections on the future of VAR, we gain a deeper appreciation for the complexities and challenges inherent in the ongoing evolution of football officiating. As VAR continues to redefine the boundaries of technology and tradition, its ultimate impact on the sport remains uncertain. Yet, amidst the debates and controversies, one thing is clear: the journey of VAR is far from over, and the future of football officiating promises to be as fascinating as it is unpredictable.

Refinement and Improvement: Addressing Criticisms

In this chapter, we confront the criticisms and challenges that have plagued Video Assistant Refereeing (VAR) since its inception, exploring the ongoing efforts to refine and improve the technology in response to feedback from stakeholders within the footballing community.

Enhancing Consistency: One of the primary criticisms of VAR has been its perceived lack of consistency in decision-making. We examine how footballing authorities are addressing this issue through improved training and education for referees and VAR officials, as well as the development of standardized protocols and guidelines for VAR implementation. By promoting greater uniformity in officiating decisions, these initiatives aim to enhance the credibility and integrity of VAR.

Streamlining Decision-Making: Another criticism of VAR has been the perceived delays and disruptions to the flow of matches caused by lengthy review processes. We analyze how technological advancements, such as improved video review systems and streamlined communication protocols, are being implemented to expedite decision-making and minimize interruptions during matches. Through the optimization of VAR workflows and procedures, footballing authorities seek to strike a balance between accuracy and efficiency in officiating.

Transparency and Communication: Critics have also raised concerns about the transparency and communication surrounding VAR decisions, particularly regarding the rationale behind overturned calls. We explore how footballing authorities are addressing these concerns through increased transparency in VAR decision-making, including the public release of VAR review footage and the publication of detailed explanations for controversial decisions. By fostering greater openness and accountability, these measures aim to rebuild trust and confidence in VAR among fans, players, and coaches alike.

Evolving Technology: As technology continues to evolve, so too does the potential for VAR to refine and improve its capabilities. We examine the ongoing research and development efforts aimed at harnessing emerging technologies, such as artificial intelligence and machine learning, to enhance the accuracy and efficiency of VAR systems. By leveraging the power of data analytics and predictive modeling, these advancements hold the promise of revolutionizing football officiating and further reducing the margin for error in decision-making.

Through these initiatives and innovations, we gain a deeper understanding of the iterative nature of VAR refinement and improvement. As football authorities continue to listen to feedback, experiment with new technologies, and implement best practices, the future of VAR promises to be one of continuous evolution and innovation.

VAR in International Competitions: Challenges and Opportunities

In this chapter, we explore the unique challenges and opportunities presented by the implementation of Video Assistant Refereeing (VAR) in international football competitions, where the stakes are higher and the scrutiny is intensified.

Global Standardization: International competitions bring together teams from diverse footballing cultures and regions, each with its own interpretation of the laws of the game. We examine the challenges of implementing VAR in international competitions and the efforts to establish global standards and protocols for VAR implementation. From coordinating with multiple national federations to training and certifying VAR officials from around the world, footballing authorities strive to promote consistency and fairness in officiating across international competitions.

Cultural Sensitivity: VAR's introduction to international competitions also raises cultural and logistical challenges that must be navigated sensitively. We explore how footballing authorities balance the need for technological innovation with respect for the traditions and customs of participating teams and fans. From addressing language barriers to accommodating diverse officiating styles and preferences, efforts are made to ensure that VAR enhances – rather than disrupts – the spirit and integrity of international football.

High-Stakes Decisions: The high-stakes nature of international competitions amplifies the pressure and scrutiny surrounding VAR decisions. We analyze how the potential impact of VAR on match outcomes heightens the tension and drama of international tournaments, from decisive knockout matches to closely contested group-stage encounters. Through case studies and real-world examples, we illustrate the profound implications of VAR on the fortunes of nations and the emotions of fans during international competitions.

Showcase for Innovation: Despite the challenges, international competitions also provide a platform for showcasing the innovative potential of VAR on the global stage. We explore how international tournaments serve as testing grounds for new VAR technologies and protocols, from experimental rule changes to advancements in video review systems. By leveraging the visibility and prestige of international football, footballing authorities seek to drive forward the evolution and refinement of VAR on a global scale.

Through these discussions, we gain a deeper appreciation for the complexities and opportunities inherent in the implementation of VAR in international competitions. As football authorities navigate the challenges and harness the potential of VAR on the global stage, the future of international football officiating promises to be shaped by innovation, collaboration, and a commitment to excellence.

Predicting the Next Evolution: VAR 2.0 and Beyond

In this final chapter, we embark on a speculative journey into the future of Video Assistant Refereeing (VAR), envisioning the potential trajectory of VAR 2.0 and beyond as technology continues to evolve and football authorities seek to refine and improve officiating standards.

Enhanced Automation: We explore the potential for increased automation in VAR decision-making, leveraging advancements in artificial intelligence and machine learning to automate certain aspects of the review process. From real-time analysis of video footage to predictive modeling of offside calls and fouls, VAR 2.0 could usher in a new era of efficiency and accuracy in football officiating.

Augmented Reality Integration: We examine how augmented reality (AR) technology may be integrated into VAR systems, providing referees with enhanced visualizations and overlays to aid decision-making. From virtual lines for offside calls to holographic replays for contentious incidents, AR could revolutionize the way referees review and adjudicate on-field incidents in real-time.

Fan Engagement and Interaction: VAR 2.0 could also usher in new opportunities for fan engagement and interaction, leveraging technology to provide fans with unprecedented access to VAR decision-making processes. We explore the potential for immersive fan experiences, such as virtual reality (VR) simulations of VAR reviews and interactive decision-making platforms that allow fans to participate in the officiating process in real-time.

Ethical and Regulatory Considerations: As VAR technology continues to evolve, we must also consider the ethical and regulatory implications of its implementation. We examine the potential challenges and controversies that may arise from increased automation and augmented reality integration, from concerns about data privacy to questions of accountability and transparency in decision-making.

Collaborative Innovation: Finally, we envision a future where footballing authorities, technology developers, and stakeholders collaborate to drive forward the evolution of VAR. Through open dialogue, experimentation, and shared best practices, VAR 2.0 and beyond have the potential to shape the future of football officiating in ways that enhance the integrity, fairness, and excitement of the beautiful game.

Through these speculative predictions, we gain a glimpse into the exciting possibilities that lie ahead for VAR and the future of football officiating. As technology continues to evolve and football authorities embrace innovation, the journey of VAR promises to be one of continuous evolution and advancement, shaping the future of the sport for generations to come.

BEYOND THE PITCH

In this concluding section, we broaden our perspective to explore the wider implications and impact of Video Assistant Refereeing (VAR) beyond the confines of the football pitch.

Societal Impact: We examine how VAR's introduction to football reflects broader societal trends and developments, from the increasing reliance on technology in daily life to the growing demand for transparency and accountability in public institutions. By analyzing VAR's influence on public perceptions of fairness and justice, we gain insights into the evolving relationship between technology, sport, and society.

Technological Innovation: The adoption of VAR represents a milestone in the ongoing evolution of technology in sport. We explore how VAR's implementation has spurred technological innovation and research in fields such as computer vision, data analytics, and artificial intelligence. By examining the synergies between sport and technology, we uncover the potential for cross-disciplinary collaboration and knowledge-sharing to drive forward the frontiers of innovation in both domains.

Global Connectivity: VAR's introduction has also facilitated greater connectivity and engagement among football fans around the world. We analyze how VAR-related discussions and debates transcend geographical boundaries, uniting fans from diverse cultures and backgrounds in shared conversations and experiences. By harnessing the power of digital media and social platforms, VAR has transformed football into a truly global phenomenon, fostering a sense of community and camaraderie among fans worldwide.

Ethical and Moral Considerations: VAR's implementation raises important ethical and moral questions about the intersection of technology and sport. We examine the implications of VAR's use of video technology for privacy, surveillance, and data ethics, as well as the potential for bias and discrimination in decision-making processes. By critically assessing VAR's impact on society, we can better understand its role in shaping broader debates about fairness, justice, and accountability in the digital age.

Future Directions: Looking ahead, we speculate on the potential future directions of VAR and its implications for the future of sport and society. From advancements in technology and regulation to shifts in cultural attitudes and values, we explore the dynamic interplay between VAR and the forces shaping the world around us. By envisioning different scenarios and possibilities, we can better prepare for the challenges and opportunities that lie ahead in the ever-changing landscape of sport and technology.

Through this holistic exploration of VAR's impact beyond the pitch, we gain a deeper appreciation for the multifaceted nature of its influence on sport, society, and the human experience. As we navigate the complexities of VAR's implementation and evolution, we are reminded of the broader implications of technological innovation in shaping the future of sport and society.

Officiating Ethics and Integrity

In this chapter, we delve into the ethical considerations and principles that underpin the role of officiating in football, exploring how Video

Assistant Refereeing (VAR) intersects with issues of fairness, integrity, and accountability.

Upholding Fair Play: We examine the fundamental principle of fair play in football officiating and its implications for VAR implementation. From the importance of impartiality and objectivity in decision-making to the need for consistency and transparency in officiating processes, we explore how VAR is reshaping perceptions of fairness and justice on the pitch.

Maintaining Integrity: Integrity lies at the heart of officiating ethics, encompassing honesty, impartiality, and ethical conduct. We analyze how VAR's introduction has raised questions about the integrity of officiating, from concerns about the potential for bias or favoritism to the challenges of maintaining public trust and confidence in officiating decisions.

Accountability and Transparency: VAR's implementation has prompted calls for greater accountability and transparency in officiating, with stakeholders demanding clarity and justification for VAR decisions. We explore the mechanisms for accountability in VAR, from post-match reviews and assessments to public disclosures of VAR protocols and procedures. By promoting openness and transparency, football authorities seek to enhance the credibility and integrity of VAR officiating.

Ethical Dilemmas and Challenges: VAR's introduction has also brought to light ethical dilemmas and challenges that must be navigated by officials and stakeholders. We examine issues such as the balance between technological innovation and traditional officiating principles, the ethical implications of VAR's use in contentious decisions, and the potential for unintended consequences in decision-making processes.

Continuing Education and Training: As VAR continues to evolve, ongoing education and training are essential to ensure that officials uphold the highest ethical standards in their officiating duties. We explore the importance of continuous professional development for referees and VAR officials, including training on ethical decision-making, conflict resolution, and cultural sensitivity.

Through these discussions, we gain a deeper understanding of the ethical dimensions of officiating in the VAR era. By grappling with issues of fairness, integrity, and accountability, we reaffirm the importance of upholding ethical principles in football officiating and preserving the integrity of the beautiful game.

Financial Implications: VAR's Impact on Clubs and Leagues

In this chapter, we delve into the financial ramifications of Video Assistant Refereeing (VAR) implementation on football clubs and leagues, exploring both the costs and benefits associated with the adoption of this technology.

Initial Investment: We analyze the significant upfront costs incurred by clubs and leagues for the installation and implementation of VAR systems. From investing in high-definition cameras and video review equipment to retrofitting stadiums with VAR infrastructure, the initial capital outlay for VAR implementation can be substantial, especially for smaller clubs and lower-tier leagues.

Operational Expenses: Beyond the initial investment, VAR systems also entail ongoing operational expenses for maintenance, personnel, and training. We examine the staffing requirements for VAR operations, including the recruitment and training of VAR officials, as well as the costs associated with equipment maintenance, software updates, and technical support services.

Impact on Revenue Streams: While VAR implementation represents a significant financial burden for clubs and leagues, it also has the potential to impact revenue streams in various ways. We explore how VAR-induced controversies and debates may affect fan engagement and attendance, potentially impacting ticket sales, merchandise revenue, and sponsorship opportunities. Conversely, the increased accuracy and integrity of officiating facilitated by VAR may enhance the commercial appeal of the sport, attracting new audiences and investment opportunities.

Insurance and Liability: VAR's introduction has also prompted clubs and leagues to reassess their insurance and liability coverage in light of potential VAR-related disputes and claims. We examine how clubs and leagues may need to adjust their insurance policies to mitigate the financial risks associated with VAR-induced controversies, including legal expenses and compensation claims from aggrieved parties.

Long-Term Viability: Despite the initial financial challenges posed by VAR implementation, we consider its long-term viability and potential return on investment for clubs and leagues. Through cost-benefit analyses and economic modeling, we assess the net impact of VAR on club finances and league revenues over time, weighing the benefits of improved officiating accuracy and integrity against the costs of implementation and operation.

Through these discussions, we gain a comprehensive understanding of the financial implications of VAR's impact on football clubs and leagues. By analyzing the costs and benefits associated with VAR implementation, clubs and leagues can make informed decisions about the role of technology in shaping the future of the sport while safeguarding their financial sustainability and competitiveness.

Societal Reflections: VAR's Influence on Fan Culture and Football Discourse

In this chapter, we explore the broader societal implications of Video Assistant Refereeing (VAR), examining its influence on fan culture and football discourse in the digital age.

Shifting Fan Narratives: We analyze how VAR has reshaped fan narratives and discourse surrounding football, sparking debates and discussions on social media platforms, fan forums, and digital communities. From heated arguments over controversial decisions to nuanced discussions about the role of technology in officiating, VAR has become a focal point for fan engagement and interaction, shaping the collective identity and culture of football fandom.

Impact on Matchday Experience: The introduction of VAR has also had a tangible impact on the matchday experience for fans, both in stadiums and at home. We explore how VAR-induced delays and disruptions have affected the rhythm and atmosphere of matches, as well as the emotional rollercoaster experienced by fans as they await the outcome of VAR reviews. Through surveys and interviews, we capture the diverse range of perspectives and reactions among fans to VAR's influence on the live footballing experience.

Amplifying Voices: VAR's introduction has amplified the voices of fans and stakeholders in the footballing community, empowering them to participate in officiating discussions and debates like never before. We examine how social media platforms and digital technologies have democratized football discourse, providing fans with a platform to express their opinions, share insights, and hold officiating authorities accountable for VAR-related decisions.

Cultivating Critical Thinking: VAR's presence has also cultivated a culture of critical thinking and analysis among fans, encouraging them to question officiating decisions and engage in reasoned debate about the nuances of VAR implementation. We explore how fans have become more discerning and analytical in their assessments of VAR-related incidents, drawing on video replays, statistical analysis, and expert commentary to form informed opinions about the impact of technology on the sport.

Bridging Divides: Despite the controversies and debates surrounding VAR, it has also served as a unifying force, bridging divides and bringing fans together in shared experiences and conversations. We examine how VAR-induced controversies transcend tribal allegiances and rivalries, fostering a sense of camaraderie and solidarity among fans as they navigate the complexities of modern officiating together.

Through these reflections on VAR's influence on fan culture and football discourse, we gain a deeper appreciation for its profound impact on the social fabric of the beautiful game. As VAR continues to shape the way fans engage with football, it serves as a testament to the enduring power of technology to transform the sport and enrich the lives of fans around the world.

CONCLUSION

In this book, we have embarked on a comprehensive exploration of Video Assistant Refereeing (VAR) in football, delving into its origins, evolution, implementation, and impact on the sport at every level. From the intricacies of VAR technology to its profound implications for officiating, tactics, fan culture, and beyond, we have uncovered the multifaceted dimensions of VAR's influence on the beautiful game.

Throughout our journey, we have encountered a myriad of perspectives, opinions, and insights from stakeholders across the footballing community – from players and managers to referees, fans, and administrators. We have grappled with the challenges and controversies that have accompanied VAR's introduction, from debates over its impact on the flow and rhythm of matches to concerns about its potential to undermine the human element of officiating.

Yet, amidst the controversies and complexities, one thing is clear: VAR represents a transformative force in football, reshaping the way the game is played, officiated, and experienced by millions of fans around the world. Whether through its potential to enhance officiating accuracy and fairness, spark debates and discussions among fans, or drive technological innovation in the sport, VAR has left an indelible mark on the fabric of football.

As we conclude our exploration of VAR, we are reminded that the journey is far from over. The evolution of VAR continues, with ongoing advancements in technology, regulation, and best practices shaping its future trajectory. As footballing authorities, clubs, and leagues navigate the opportunities and challenges presented by VAR, they must remain vigilant in upholding the core values of the sport – fairness, integrity, and respect – while harnessing the potential of technology to enhance the beautiful game for generations to come.

In closing, we extend our gratitude to all those who have contributed to this book – the players, coaches, referees, fans, and officials whose passion and dedication fuel the spirit of football, and whose voices enrich our understanding of VAR and its impact on the sport we love. May the journey of VAR continue to inspire, provoke, and unite us in our shared love of the beautiful game.

Lessons Learned: Reflecting on VAR's Journey

In this final section, we distill the key lessons gleaned from the journey of Video Assistant Refereeing (VAR) in football, reflecting on its evolution, challenges, and impact on the sport.

Embrace Innovation with Caution: The introduction of VAR serves as a reminder of the transformative power of technology in football. While VAR has the potential to enhance officiating accuracy and fairness, its implementation has also raised complex challenges and controversies. As footballing authorities and stakeholders continue to navigate the intricacies of VAR, they must approach innovation with caution, balancing the benefits of technological advancement with the preservation of the sport's core values and traditions.

Strive for Consistency and Transparency: One of the central challenges of VAR implementation lies in achieving consistency and transparency in officiating decisions. As VAR systems evolve and protocols are refined, footballing authorities must prioritize efforts to promote uniformity and clarity in VAR decision-making processes. By fostering greater consistency and transparency, they can enhance the credibility and integrity of VAR officiating while maintaining public trust and confidence in the sport.

Engage Stakeholders in Dialogue: The journey of VAR underscores the importance of engaging stakeholders in open dialogue and collaboration. From players and coaches to referees and fans, the diverse perspectives and insights of footballing communities are essential for shaping the future of VAR. By fostering inclusive discussions and soliciting feedback from all stakeholders, footballing authorities can ensure that VAR implementation reflects the needs and aspirations of the broader footballing community.

Adapt and Evolve Over Time: VAR's journey is characterized by ongoing adaptation and evolution in response to feedback and experience. As technology advances and best practices emerge, footballing authorities must remain flexible and agile in their approach to VAR implementation. By continuously learning from successes and setbacks, they can refine VAR systems and protocols to meet the evolving needs and challenges of the sport.

Preserve the Human Element: Amidst the technological innovations of VAR, it is essential to preserve the human element of officiating in football. While VAR systems can enhance decision-making accuracy, they must complement – rather than replace – the judgment and intuition of on-field officials. By striking the right balance between technology and human judgment, footballing authorities can ensure that VAR enhances – rather than detracts from – the essence and spirit of the beautiful game.

As we reflect on the journey of VAR in football, we are reminded that its impact extends far beyond the confines of the pitch. From sparking debates and discussions among fans to driving technological innovation in the sport, VAR's influence resonates throughout the footballing community. By embracing the lessons learned from VAR's journey, we can navigate the challenges and opportunities of the future with wisdom, humility, and a shared commitment to the enduring values of football.

Looking Ahead: Anticipating the Next Chapter in Football's Technological Evolution

In this final chapter, we cast our gaze forward, envisioning the next chapter in football's technological evolution beyond Video Assistant Refereeing (VAR). As we stand at the intersection of sport and technology, we anticipate the emergence of new innovations and trends that will shape the future of football in the digital age.

Advanced Officiating Technologies: Building on the foundation laid by VAR, we anticipate the development of even more sophisticated officiating technologies that leverage artificial intelligence, machine learning, and real-time data analytics. From automated offside detection systems to predictive foul recognition algorithms, these advancements hold the promise of further enhancing the accuracy and efficiency of officiating in football.

Immersive Fan Experiences: The future of football will be characterized by immersive fan experiences that blur the boundaries between the virtual and the real. We envision the integration of augmented reality (AR) and virtual reality (VR) technologies into live matches, allowing fans to experience the action from new perspectives and interact with players and officials in unprecedented ways. From interactive VR broadcasts to AR-enhanced stadium experiences, the possibilities for fan engagement are limitless.

Data-Driven Performance Analysis: As technology continues to revolutionize the way football is played and coached, we anticipate the widespread adoption of data-driven performance analysis tools that provide insights and recommendations based on real-time data. From wearable sensors that track player movements and biometrics to predictive analytics platforms that forecast match outcomes and tactical strategies, the era of data-driven football is upon us.

Sustainable Innovations: In an era of increasing environmental awareness and sustainability concerns, we anticipate the emergence of eco-friendly innovations that minimize the carbon footprint of football stadiums and operations. From renewable energy solutions to sustainable materials and construction practices, footballing authorities and clubs will prioritize environmental stewardship as they build the stadiums of tomorrow.

Ethical and Social Considerations: As football embraces new technologies, it must also grapple with ethical and social considerations that arise from their use. From concerns about data privacy and security to questions of fairness and equity in access to technological innovations, footballing authorities must navigate the complexities of the digital age with integrity and responsibility.

As we embark on this journey into the future of football's technological evolution, we are reminded of the timeless values that underpin the beautiful game – teamwork, passion, and camaraderie. While technology may shape the way football is played, officiated, and experienced, it is the spirit of the sport and the love of the game that will endure for generations to come. As we anticipate the next chapter in football's technological evolution, let us embrace the future with optimism, curiosity, and a shared commitment to advancing the beautiful game for all.

Final Thoughts: Balancing Tradition with Progress in the Beautiful Game

As we conclude our exploration of Video Assistant Refereeing (VAR) and its impact on football, we are reminded of the delicate balance between tradition and progress in the beautiful game. Football is a sport steeped in rich history and tradition, yet it is also a dynamic and evolving phenomenon that reflects the zeitgeist of the times.

VAR represents a significant leap forward in the evolution of football officiating, harnessing technology to enhance the accuracy, fairness, and integrity of decision-making on the pitch. Yet, its introduction has also sparked debates and controversies that challenge the traditions and conventions of the sport.

In navigating the complexities of VAR implementation, footballing authorities, clubs, and stakeholders must strive to strike a balance between embracing innovation and preserving the essence of the game. While technology has the power to enhance officiating accuracy and fan engagement, it must complement – rather than overshadow – the human element of football.

At its core, football is a sport of passion, emotion, and camaraderie – values that transcend the boundaries of time and technology. As we embrace the opportunities and challenges of the digital age, let us remain rooted in the traditions and values that have defined football for generations.

In the ever-changing landscape of football, let us remember that it is the spirit of the game – the joy of competition, the thrill of victory, and the camaraderie of the fans – that truly makes football a beautiful game. As we continue on this journey of innovation and progress, let us do so with reverence for the traditions of the past and a commitment to preserving the magic of football for future generations to enjoy.

In the end, it is this delicate balance between tradition and progress that ensures football remains not just a sport, but a timeless and cherished cultural phenomenon that unites people around the world in the shared love of the beautiful game.

Printed in Great Britain
by Amazon